Secrets to
Making Love Last

By Amy Secret

Secrets to Making Love Last

By Amy Secret

Introduction

For over two decades I have worked as an Occupational Therapist specializing in the care of geriatric patients. During this time, I have had the privilege and honor of treating thousands of amazing people. As a medical professional who traveled for work, I was able to develop close connections with people from all over the United States. Often, I would meet couples; one spouse/partner requiring my services, and the other attending the treatments to offer support. Noticing these couples had a special bond, I found myself curious, asking, "What is the secret to making love last?"

This book is a compilation of years of interviews from couples willing to share their answer. My hope and intention for this book is to pass along those secrets to you.

I wish you both a lifetime full of lasting love and happiness.

Amy Secret

Dedication

This book is dedicated to my father, F. Pete Secret,the biggest supporter of my never ending, out there, and sometimes crazy, projects. To date, he is also the biggest financial supporter of Support Orphans in Morocco. His generous financial support is responsible for making this book possible.

This book is also dedicated to my brother's son, Blake Secret and his bride, Kate McQuilken. Way back in 1995, the first edition of this book was dedicated to his parents on their wedding day. It gives me enormous pleasure to share this book, once again, with the next generation of my family.

A Special Note of
Interest and Appreciation

Since March 1, 2021, I have been a volunteer in Morocco. Proceeds from this book will go to help fund the volunteer program at Child House orphanage in Essaouira, Morocco.

The Wednesday class is responsible for the artwork in this book:

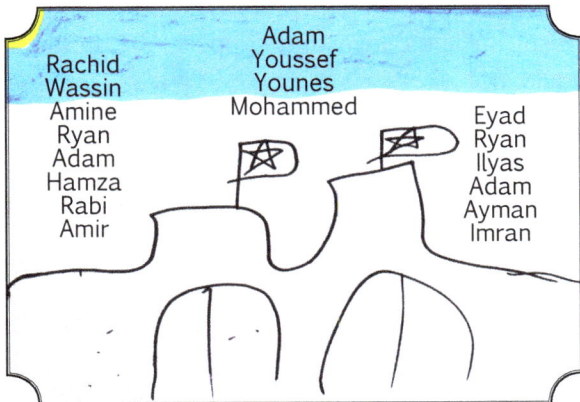

Rachid
Wassin
Amine
Ryan
Adam
Hamza
Rabi
Amir

Adam
Youssef
Younes
Mohammed

Eyad
Ryan
Ilyas
Adam
Ayman
Imran

Additional thanks go to the other volunteers who make Wednesdays at the orphanage so special: Marianne Boers from Holland, June Marantos from Canada, Jane Buckler from United Kingdom, and Nicola Happle from United Kingdom.

A huge thank you to Ana Arango ana@anaarango.com and Gaël Farano gfarano.espresso@gmail.com. Without their artistic abilities, love and support, this book would not exist.

If you would like information on how you can contribute to Child House orphanage, please contact me on Facebook: Amy Dominica-Secret.

"Don't have a lot of friends.
Keep your family close and
focus on them.
Keep outside influences at bay."
47 years

❖ ◇ ❖

"We still like each other."
48 years

⸻◇⸻

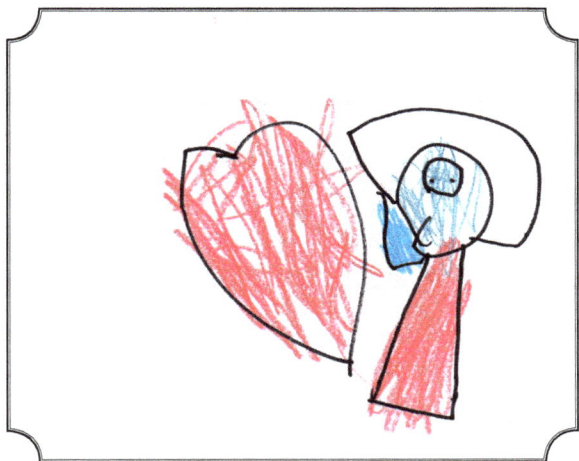

"It takes a lot of
compromising."
20 years

"No one knows
when we are mad.
In other words,
we don't air
our dirty laundry."
41 years

———◇———

"He loves me, and I love him;
we don't fight, fuss or cuss."
53 years

"Know that some days
you will be the light
for your partner and
some days your partner
will be the light for you.
No one person can carry the
light all the time. Both partners
must be committed to sharing
that privilege. As long
as there is light,
there is hope and a way."
46 years

"Forgiveness is a choice. When one person forgives, two are healed. There is no love without forgiveness and no forgiveness without love".
46 years

"I picked a good man
-just work together."
55 years

"My advice to
any newly married couple
is to never go
to bed angry."
46 years

———◇———◇———◇———

"Above all, remember to be patient and kind."
50 years

"My wife is always right."
28 years

"Learn to be secure
in insecurity."
46 years

———◇—◇—◇———

"When looking for a partner, find someone who will be your teammate."
22 years

"There is no secret
to a long-lasting marriage.
It is just about getting along."
52 years

"The first 25 years
we did it his way.
The second 25 years
we did it my way.
After 50 years
we aren't concerned
with whose way we do it."
50 years

———◇———◇———◇———

"We still like each other."
48 years

———⟡——◇——⟡———

"When you get
into a disagreement,
ask yourself this;
What is more important?
My point of view or
my spouse's feelings?"
42 years

—⬦—◇—⬦—

"It's all about love."
43 years

———◇———◇———◇———

"The secret to a long- lasting
marriage is patience, love
and doing things for
the other person
because you want to...
you have to want to."
30 years

——⟡——◇——⟡——

"It's simple.
Two remote controls."
48 years

———◇———◇———◇———

"Learn to be friends
before you love each other."
36 years

—◇——◇——◇—

BUAN

"We believe
that both people
need to see
the relationship
as a partnership."
41 years

———◇———◇———◇———

"My advice to anyone
considering marriage is this...
go into it realistically,
you'll have a much better
chance of survival."
32 years

"You can choose to be right,
or you can choose
to be happy."
45 years

———◇———◇———◇———

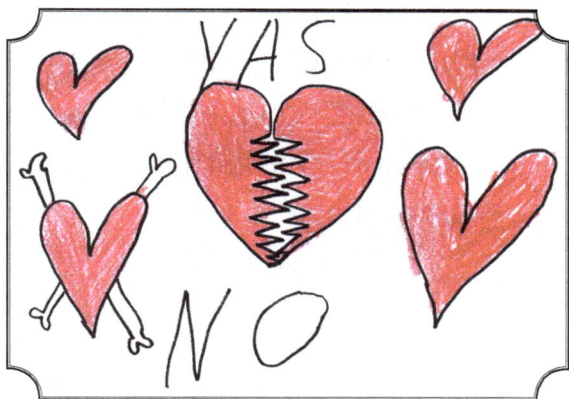

"Trust is huge. Trust means that no matter what you can count on the other to be there. If you don't have trust, you don't have anything."
50 years

"For better and for worse is real. When you sign up to be with someone, it's best to expect that your relationship will go through lots of ups and downs. It is best to know this going into your relationship. Real love isn't Hollywood love."
52 years

"Respect each other.
Never correct
your partner
in the presence
of others."
38 years

⸺⟡⸺◇⸺⟡⸺

"Stick with it
and work hard at it."
40 years

"It's simple, just
love each other.
Don't answer each other back."
66 years

———◇———

"Remember,
once you say something
(particularly during an argument)
it's out there forever."
10 years

—◇—◇—◇—

"Be independent enough
to have your own interests.
Yet still be able to meet
in the middle and enjoy
some things in common."
20 years

"Marriage is a two-way street.
It depends on the willingness of
two people working at it.
Don't go into it having
the illusion that it is going
to be, or is supposed to be,
easy the whole time."
52 years

"We have always lived
by the motto:
Love takes care of everything."
55 year

———◇———◇———◇———

"When we first got married,
we had the chance
to get a new bed,
bigger than our double.
We declined, our small bed
has kept us close
and cuddling for 45 years."
45 years

"We believe that
good communication
is what has kept us
going strong for 14 years."
14 years

———◇———◇———◇———

"God is an important part
of our lives as individuals
and as husband and wife."
40 years

"Every anniversary we recite
our vows to each other.
I believe that tradition has
helped keep our love
and commitment alive."
49 years

"As long as God is in your life you can have a wonderful, fulfilling marriage even through the trying times."
10 years

"Always remember
to take the time to laugh
and to play together."
55 years

"Kiss and hug as much as possible. Kiss to say hello, kiss to say good morning. Kiss to say goodbye, kiss to say goodnight."
38 years

"Make sure you are friends first. I married my best friend and I believe that is what has worked for us."
35 years

"Marriage is like a flower.
It is a living thing that needs
care, love, and attention daily.
This includes during sunny days,
thunderstorms, plentiful rain,
dry spells, and
seasonal changes."
46 years

"Be thoughtful of one another."
54 years

"Communication is the key.
A lot of arguments are because
of a simple misunderstanding.
We had to make an effort to
develop communication skills.
It wasn't always easy,
but it was worth it."
50 years

"My advice is to always put the other person first. Putting your partner first should always be your priority."
25 years

"Forgiveness is the key
and the ability to really
listen to one another until
the other feels heard.
Also, knowing two heads
are better than one
and how to compromise
are important to a successful
relationship."
46 years

"Be patient.
It is not a pleasant road
all of the time.
It takes a little of everything
to make it work."
57 years

"Marry your best friend."
45 years

———◇———◇———◇———

"Never go to bed angry."
46 years

"Say I'm sorry.
Saying you are sorry
can go a long way."
58 years

—◇—◇—◇—

"Good communication
and trust."
25 years

───◇───◇───◇───

www.ingramcontent.com/pod-product-compliance
Lightning Source LLC
Chambersburg PA
CBHW060253030426
42335CB00014B/1677